Gratitude

For each new morning with its light,
For rest and shelter of the night,
For health and food, for love and friends,
For everything Thy goodness sends.

Ralph Waldo Emerson

You Are Amazing!

In this book we'll highlight all the good things in your life and create more of them! Begin now. It's an exciting,, artful adventure!

~ ~ ~

If it feels like the world has been beating you down, this book will build you back up again!

"Finally, a book that builds confidence and self-esteem for you and your kids!"

GRATITUDE JOURNAL

(and family fun activity book)

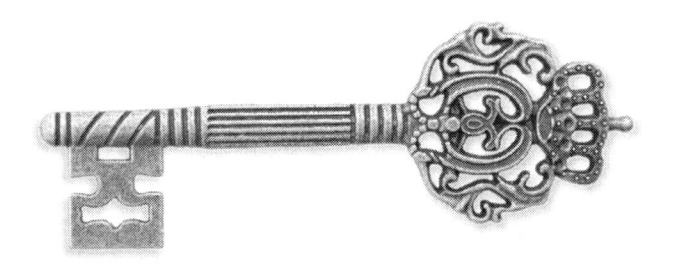

How To Feel Better, Get Better
Discover the Best Parts of You
by Asking the <u>Right</u> Questions

includes
60 MINDFUL COLORING MANDALAS & DESIGNS

ROBERT M. SCHWARZTRAUBER

Copyright 2015
by the author, Robert M. Schwarztrauber.

The author retains sole copyright to his
contributions to this book, including all photographs,
illustrations, and all text not specifically credited to another.
It is unlawful to reproduce and or redistribute, for profit or for free,
the full contents or any part of this book by ANY means without specific
written permission from the author. All copyright infringements will
be prosecuted to the full extent of the law.
(Plus, it's just not cool to steal other people's stuff.)

For more information on this, or other fine products
by this author, please visit the authors page at the end
of this book, or visit:

http://JournalOnUp.com

Find us on [f]

http://facebook.com/thegratitudedude

The Magical Power of Gratitude
How to Retrain Your Brain
To Serve, Not Fight You

I cried inside, for that little girl.
She couldn't have been more than 4 years old.

Moments before, I passed her and her mom racing each other through the park. The little girl was giggling so hard as she ran. And why not? She was beating her mom by just a hair. Mom was also laughing. They were so happy. And it warmed my heart, remembering the days when my daughters and I used to enjoy racing each other through that very same grassy field in Lincoln Park.

But as I completed my loop 'round the park, not more than five minutes time in total, the scene had changed for the worse. Much worse.

Mom was now red-faced and screaming at the daughter. "What's wrong with you!" "Why did you do that!"

And I cried inside for that poor little girl.

I don't know if this was the first time she was asked to betray herself. To search for an answer to a rhetorical question asked far too often in our society. "What is wrong with you?"

She was only 4. She thought she was helping, I'm sure she did, by closing the trunk for mom. How could she have known mom foolishly set her keys down in that trunk?

What's wrong with her? Nothing! This sweet little girl had no clue. The outcome could not be foretold. She was only 4.

But this is how it happens to us; without malice, innocently enough. Maybe we spill our milk, or drop our plate. Maybe we close the door on someone. Maybe we forgot our homework, or to take out the garbage. These are just accidents.

There is nothing "wrong" with us.

But parents, in their frustration, ask this absurd question. "What's wrong with you?"

They ask it over and over again as we grow up. Brothers and sisters join in too. Maybe teachers. Maybe "friends" and relatives. We hear it over and over until we begin to ask ourselves, "What IS wrong with me?"

Of course the only proper answer is WE ARE HUMAN. We all make mistakes. In fact, it's almost impossible to learn if we don't make mistakes! Making mistakes is a vital part of learning and growing. Oh, the irony!

Then we beat ourselves up inside searching for the answer to a question that has no valid or acceptable answer. THERE IS NOTHING WRONG WITH US!

So many lives are made smaller, more miserable by searching for what's wrong. On the flip side, so many lives are made bigger, happier by searching for the answer to the question, "What's right in my life?"

"What's RIGHT with me?"

Our brains are SO powerful. They will give us an answer to whatever question we ask it.

If we ask our brain what is good, it will find us an answer. If we ask our brain to look for red, it will search until it finds red. If we ask our brain to recall someone's name, it will continue searching for days, even as we sleep, until it can deliver an answer. The answer often comes as we are busy doing something else, like washing the dishes or taking a shower. It may take its sweet time, but the subconscious mind is always at work on our questions.

So when we ask it, "What's wrong with me?" it will get busy on finding you an answer, even to your detriment. And if it can't find a good answer, it will make one up. "Your hair is too short. Too long. You're ugly. You're too fat, too thin, too bald. You're stupid. You're in the wrong town. You're too poor. You're the rich kid." All judgments. But not one valid answer. *BECAUSE THERE IS NOTHING WRONG WITH YOU!*

We are all different. Unique. And we all have challenges to overcome, skills we can improve upon.

But we accept more quickly the bad things our brain tells us. We let it effect us. We ask it "dumb" questions and then wonder why we get down. We are biased toward negatives.

We should not waste our time and the magnificent power of our brain by asking it "dumb" questions. We should use its infinite power wisely by asking it empowering questions. By asking it questions that empower us, we can rise up and feel good. Any time we choose to.

The news channels feed us a constant supply of what is "wrong" in the world. Sadly, good news does not sell advertising and scandal brings more viewers than invention and innovation. So they bombard us with the negative. Watch or read enough news and you're bound to feel down, hopeless and depressed. Stop it. Tune out the negative.

Know that just as much right and good is going on in the world, right now, in your own home town and everywhere.

New inventions to improve our life are made daily. We live in better conditions, with better food, technology, healthcare and opportunity than any generation before us.

To feel good we just have to look for the good. We need to focus on what's RIGHT, not what's wrong.

This book will help you do just that.

YOU ARE GREAT! We all are in some way. But with all the external messages we are bombarded with each day, we often forget to recognize and appreciate the good.

We are all blessed in some way. And there is always someone who is worse off. There is someone, somewhere in the world who has tougher challenges than we do. So we should be grateful for what we have, no matter how small.

Gratitude is a habit we develop. And as we become more grateful, we begin to find and acquire more things to be grateful for. Imagine, if we do not feel and express gratitude for what we already have, how can we expect to be given more? Imagine getting a gift and not saying, "Thank you." It's unlikely you will get another.

And so it is with the universe, as far back as we can remember. Gratitude is the key that opens ourselves to the possibility for more.

TIPS for USING THIS BOOK

To get the very most from this book, to really begin to feel good about yourself and all the special and unique gifts you bring to the world, do one full page daily. It takes just a few minutes.

Most people find it helpful to do this at the end of each day.

Find a few moments before bedtime to relax and recall the events of the day. It only takes a few minutes to answer the simple questions which were designed to draw out your best.

How much better it is going to bed feeling good about yourself, rather than dwelling on and rehashing the problems of the day.

If you cannot answer all the questions, that's OK. Just do the ones which are appropriate or most relevant to that day. On the back of each daily question page you'll also find space to write anything else you wish or expand on any of your answers from the front page.

Quality Time With The Kids

You can use one page for yourself and it's incredibly fun and helpful to do a page with your children too. They love to tell you about their day and it is a great way to help them focus on the good, look for what's good, and it can help them build their confidence as you explore all that's good about them!

The coloring designs are a great bonus for relaxation and reflection as you close out the day. Your kids might love to do them and show off their talents here as well.

As you focus on what's good, as you develop the habit of being grateful for all the good things in your life, you will become ever happier and find even more to be grateful for.

I am grateful you have chosen this book. I hope using it can help you as much as it has helped me...and even more!

We need to look for what's good. We do this by asking better questions.

Asking ourselves better questions is the focus of this book. When we ask our powerful brain to search for what is good, it finds it.

"What's right with you?"

I'll bet know one has ever asked you THAT questions!

It's time to change our focus from asking negative questions to asking positive, powerful, empowering, feel-good questions.

We talk to ourselves all day long. We are constantly asking ourselves questions. When we change the inner conversation we are having in our head, we change the course of our life.

When we focus on what's good, we find more of it.

To quote from the all-time, best selling book in the world, the Bible, Matthew 7:7, "Ask, and it will be given to you; seek, and you will find; knock, and it will be opened to you. 8 "For everyone who asks receives, and he who seeks finds, and to him who knocks it will be opened....

Ask. Ask better questions. Ask what is good about you, what is great about you and you will be given the answer.

Isn't it far more enjoyable, more useful, more empowering to know what is good about you?

But sometimes, we just don't know what questions to ask. We're too modest, too humble. We're told from an early age not to brag or be boastful about ourselves. And in some situations, that is appropriate. But it is ALWAYS appropriate to talk good about ourselves TO ourselves.

If we won't talk well or think well of ourselves, who else will?

It begins with gratitude for ourselves. For our talents, our skills, our kindness, our insight, our specialized knowledge, our compassion, our wit.

We are ALL great at something. Good at something. We've all done something nice for someone, sometime. And remembering that makes us feel good. Makes us want to do good again.

When we are grateful for what we have, no matter how little that might be at this point in time, we set ourselves up to get more. Whatever we focus on we find more of. Maybe it's a backpack, clothes, or shoes. A classic one is when you buy a new car. Suddenly, you notice more of that same model car on the road than you ever did before. Because our mind has been made more aware of that. Our focus has been changed.

Luckily, we can change our focus whenever we choose.

We can choose to focus on what is good in the world, what is RIGHT in our life. We can focus on the good we have done and intend to do in the future. We can focus on the best of our abilities, the positives, rather than dwell on the negatives.

By asking ourselves better questions, more empowering, more inspiring questions we can choose to feel good about ourselves. Everyday!

In this book you'll feel your mood change daily as you answer questions about the best of you. You'll feel gratitude for the blessings and talents you already possess, but are seldom recognized for; or even think about.

You'll be reminded of how good you really are and of the value you have to share with others. This book can build your confidence to great heights.

Help Children Be Strong and Confident

If you're a parent, this book is a great way to spend quality time with your child, teaching him or her the value of being grateful for what you have, rather than always thinking you'll be happier if you just had _____.

You can give your child a solid foundation for a well adjusted and confident life.

Your child will love telling you about his day and showing you just how good and proud he or she really is. And you can reinforce all of their good points. And point out positive qualities and actions they may have missed.

Relaxation

While recounting the blessings of each day builds confidence and boosts your mood, coloring Mandalas and designs images has been shown to relax and soothe our spirit and our souls.

When we can take simple line drawings and turn them into beautiful finished artworks, we gain a great sense of satisfaction, accomplishment and instant gratification.

Mandalas are an ancient art form of Hindu or Buddhist origin which use concentric geometric shapes or designs to represent the universe and mankind's search for completeness and unity. (See pg 141 for more specific details on the mandala's power to heal and lift the spirit)

Drawing and coloring are simple acts, but their power to change us should not be underestimated. Our focus tends to be on making the big changes, and we often overlook the small daily changes that will add up to success.

Everyone has heard that old phrase, "An apple a day keeps the doctor away." There is great truth in that simple phrase. We could all be healthier if we ate more fruit. We know it. It's a simple thing we can all do.

But do we?

This book is simple by design. Answer questions about yourself. Write out goals you have. Describe things you would like to do, see, or become.

Write. Read. Draw or color. Very simple acts.

And if we can take time to do them everyday, even if we only do a little, oh what powerful changes they can bring to our life!

"By the yard it's hard. By the inch it's a cinch."

Even the largest buildings are built one brick at a time. Simple foundations lead to grand skyscrapers. Small things lead to great things.

Take one simple step today toward building the life you've always dreamed of. Focus on the best of you. Focus on your goals. Take just a small step today, and each following day, to start building a strong foundation for yourself and for the family and friends you love.

You can do it. We all can. We start small.

Let's begin this journey with a few inspirational quotes by a gentleman who greatly influences me to this day. Jim Rohn helped millions sharing his simple wisdom. He is gone now, but his words and wisdom live on.

"For things to change for you, you have to change."
"Anything that's easy to do, is easy *not* to do."
"Progress is the key to happiness"

NOTE: You will quickly notice the same or similar empowering questions are used repeatedly. This is intentional. We learn by repetition. We want to re-train your brain, your inner conversation, to be positive rather than negative. Consider, you've likely been having the same negative conversations with yourself for years. Stay with this. Do not get bored. Soon your inner conversations will be empowering ones instead!

The Power of a Plan

In a Dominican University Study validating the effectiveness of written goals, 267 participants were recruited from businesses, organizations, and business networking groups. Of this group, 149 participants actually completed the study.

These 149 final participants ranged in age from 23 to 72, with 37 males and 112 females. Participants came from the United States, Belgium, England, India, Australia and Japan and included a variety of entrepreneurs, educators, healthcare professionals, artists, attorneys, bankers, marketers, human services providers, managers, vice presidents, and directors of non-profits, and other occupations.

Participants pursued a variety of goals including (in order of frequency reported) completing a project, increasing income, increasing productivity, getting organized, enhancing performance/achievement, enhancing life balance, reducing work anxiety and learning a new skill. Examples of "completing a project" included writing a chapter of a book, updating a website, listing and selling a house, completing a strategic plan, securing a contract, hiring employees and preventing a hostile take-over.

At the end of 4 weeks, participants were asked to rate their progress and the degree to which they had accomplished their goals.

The positive effect of written goals was supported: Those who wrote their goals accomplished significantly more than those who did not write their goals.

Why is This Important?

Since it has been proven that written goals increase our chances for success, on each empowering question page I have included space at the bottom for you to write your goals. These could be short-term goals for the next day, or the next week or month. They can also be long-term goals for the next year or 5 or 10 years. It works best to write goals for short AND long term desires. Please be sure to do this exercise! It really works.

Written goals are your roadmap to a better future. They will help keep you focused and on course. Your goals can change over time, day to day even. What is important is that you are giving them thought, attention, direction. A ship never leaves port without a known destination. How can we expect to get where we are going, achieve our desires, without a plan? Write goals.

Try something new and see what you can do.
Commit to doing the right things, right now for a right life.

What's RIGHT with You?

"Better results come from asking better questions."

My Gratitude Journal

"Be present in all things and thankful for all things."
Maya Angelou

Today's Date _____ and My Mood was:

Did I make someone smile or laugh today?

How was I kind today?

How did I help someone or something today, even in a small way?

What did I give today? Could be your time, knowledge, money, love, etc.

Today I am very grateful for having this person in my life and why:

I learned something new today:

Did I thank someone today? Who should I surprise by sending a card?

Of all the things I saw today the best by far was this:

I gave someone this compliment today:

I am looking forward to this (it's OK if it's the same as yesterday!):

I would like to help:

Who or what made me smile today?

I think this would be fun to try...and maybe a bit scary:

Today I am grateful for: (pick anything; health, wealth, wisdom, fun, a feeling)

Focusing, my goal going forward is to:

Day by day, in every way I'm getting better and better.

Creative Space

PET FRIENDLY

A little quiet time alone with our thoughts can help our brain to calm and focus. Use this Creative Space to write out thoughts or ideas you have (don't judge thoughts or ideas as good or bad, just free-think, you can even write the craziest things you can think of!) Drawing or coloring has been shown to have a therapeutic, calming effect too.

Day by day, in every way I'm getting better and better.

My Gratitude Journal

I don't have to chase extraordinary moments to find happiness - it's right in front of me if I'm paying attention and practicing gratitude.   Brene Brown

Today's Date _____ and My Mood was

I'm super-good at:

I am so lucky I can, or get to:

What I am most proud of is:

Thinking of _____ makes me feel good.

My favorite thing about Me is my:

Today, I'm glad that I:

I'm grateful for:

What I love about _____ is:

This made me happy today:

_____ always makes me smile.

I would like to help:

If I lost everything else, I'd still be grateful for:

My favorite _____ is _____ because

Today, I'm most grateful for:

Remembering, My goal going forward is to:

Day by day, in every way I'm getting better and better.   23

Creative Space

A little quiet time alone with our thoughts can help our brain to calm and focus. Use this Creative Space to write out thoughts or ideas you have (don't judge thoughts or ideas as good or bad, just free-think, you can even write the craziest things you can think of!) Drawing or coloring has been shown to have a therapeutic, calming effect too.

Day by day, in every way I'm getting better and better.

My Gratitude Journal

"Acknowledging the good that you already have in your life is the foundation for all abundance." — Eckhart Tolle

Today's Date _____ and My Mood was

How was I kind today?

Who or what made me smile today?

I learned something new today:

Did I make someone smile or laugh today?

How did I help someone/something today, even in a small way?

What did I give today? Could be your time, knowledge, money, love, etc.

Today I am very grateful for having this person in my life and why:

Did I thank someone today? Who should I surprise by sending a card?

Of all the things I saw today the best by far was this:

I gave someone this compliment today:

I am looking forward to this (it's OK if it's the same as yesterday!):

I would like to learn:

I think this would be fun to try and maybe a bit scary:

Today I am most grateful for:

Focusing, my goal going forward is to:

Day by day, in every way I'm getting better and better.

Creative Space

A little quiet time alone with our thoughts can help our brain to calm and focus. Use this Creative Space to write out thoughts or ideas you have (don't judge thoughts or ideas as good or bad, just free-think, you can even write the craziest things you can think of!) Drawing or coloring has been shown to have a therapeutic, calming effect too.

Day by day, in every way I'm getting better and better.

My Gratitude Journal

"Gratitude is not only the greatest of virtues, but the parent of all others."
Marcus Tullius Cicero

Today's Date _____ and My Mood was

This made me happy today:

I'm super-good at:

I am so lucky I can, or get to:

One of my favorite people in the world is _____ because:

Thinking of _____ makes me feel good.

My favorite thing about Me is my:

Today, I'm glad that I:

A funny thing happened today:

What I love about _____ is:

_____ always makes me smile.

I would like to help:

If I lost everything else, I'd still be grateful for:

My favorite _____ is _____ because

Today, I'm most grateful for:

Remembering, My goal going forward is to:

Day by day, in every way I'm getting better and better.

Creative Space

A little quiet time alone with our thoughts can help our brain to calm and focus. Use this Creative Space to write out thoughts or ideas you have (don't judge thoughts or ideas as good or bad, just free-think, you can even write the craziest things you can think of!) Drawing or coloring has been shown to have a therapeutic, calming effect too.

Day by day, in every way I'm getting better and better.

My Gratitude Journal

"Feeling gratitude and not expressing it is like wrapping a present and not giving it."
William Arthur Ward

Today's Date _____ and My Mood was

Who or what made me smile today?

Did I make someone smile or laugh today?

How was I kind today?

How did I help someone/something today, even in a small way?

What did I give today? Could be your time, knowledge, money, love, etc.

Today I am very grateful for having this person in my life and why:

I learned something new today:

Did I thank someone today? Who should I surprise by sending a card?

Of all the things I saw today the best by far was this:

I gave someone this compliment today:

I am looking forward to this (it's OK if it's the same as yesterday!):

I would like to help:

I think this would be fun to try and maybe a bit scary:

Today I am grateful for: Anything, health, wealth, wisdom, fun, a feeling

Remembering that my goal is to:

Day by day, in every way I'm getting better and better.

Creative Space

A little quiet time alone with our thoughts can help our brain to calm and focus. Use this Creative Space to write out thoughts or ideas you have (don't judge thoughts or ideas as good or bad, just free-think, you can even write the craziest things you can think of!) Drawing or coloring has been shown to have a therapeutic, calming effect too.

Day by day, in every way I'm getting better and better.

My Gratitude Journal

"An attitude of gratitude brings great things."
Yogi Bhajan

Today's Date _____ and My Mood was

I'm grateful for:

This made me happy today:

I have a talent for:

I am so lucky I can, or get to:

What I am most proud of is:

Thinking of _____ makes me feel good.

My favorite thing about Me is my:

Today, it made me happy when I:

What I love about _____ is:

_____ always makes me smile.

I would like to help:

If I lost everything else, I'd still be grateful for:

My favorite _____ is _____ because

Today, I'm most grateful for:

Remembering, My goal going forward is to:

Day by day, in every way I'm getting better and better.

Creative Space

A little quiet time alone with our thoughts can help our brain to calm and focus. Use this Creative Space to write out thoughts or ideas you have (don't judge thoughts or ideas as good or bad, just free-think, you can even write the craziest things you can think of!) Drawing or coloring has been shown to have a therapeutic, calming effect too.

Day by day, in every way I'm getting better and better.

Be Thankful

Be thankful that you don't already have everything you desire,
If you did, what would there be to look forward to?

Be thankful when you don't know something
For it gives you the opportunity to learn.

Be thankful for the difficult times.
During those times you grow.

Be thankful for your limitations
Because they give you opportunities for improvement.

Be thankful for each new challenge
Because it will build your strength and character.

Be thankful for your mistakes
They will teach you valuable lessons.

Be thankful when you're tired and weary
Because it means you've made a difference.

It is easy to be thankful for the good things.
A life of rich fulfillment comes to those who are
also thankful for the setbacks.

GRATITUDE can turn a negative into a positive.
Find a way to be thankful for your troubles
and they can become your blessings.

Author Unknown

Day by day, in every way I'm getting better and better.

Creative Space

A little quiet time alone with our thoughts can help our brain to calm and focus. Use this Creative Space to write out thoughts or ideas you have (don't judge thoughts or ideas as good or bad, just free-think, you can even write the craziest things you can think of!) Drawing or coloring has been shown to have a therapeutic, calming effect too.

Day by day, in every way I'm getting better and better.

My Gratitude Journal

"When you are grateful, fear disappears and abundance appears."
Anthony Robbins

Today's Date _____ and My Mood was

I learned something new today:

How was I kind today?

Who or what made me smile today?

Did I make someone smile or laugh today?

How did I help someone/something today, even in a small way?

What did I give today? (time, knowledge, money, love, etc.)

Today I am very grateful for having this person in my life and why:

Did I thank someone today? Who should I surprise by sending a card?

Of all the things I saw today the best by far was this:

I gave someone this compliment today:

I am looking forward to this (it's OK if it's the same as yesterday!):

I would like to help:

I think this would be fun to try and maybe a bit scary:

Today I am grateful for:

I am focused now on this GOAL:

Day by day, in every way I'm getting better and better.

Creative Space

A little quiet time alone with our thoughts can help our brain to calm and focus. Use this Creative Space to write out thoughts or ideas you have (don't judge thoughts or ideas as good or bad, just free-think, you can even write the craziest things you can think of!) Drawing or coloring has been shown to have a therapeutic, calming effect too.

Day by day, in every way I'm getting better and better.

My Gratitude Journal

"If the only prayer you said was thank you, that would be enough."
Meister Eckhart

Today's Date _____ and My Mood was

I'm super-good at:

I am so lucky I can, or get to:

What I like about _____ is:

What I am most proud of is:

My favorite thing about Me is my:

Today, I smiled because

I'm grateful for:

This made me happy today:

_____ always makes me smile.

I would like to help:

When I think of _____ it makes me feel good.

If I lost everything else, I'd still be grateful for:

My favorite _____ is _____ because

Today, I'm most grateful for:

Remembering, My goal going forward is to:

Day by day, in every way I'm getting better and better.

Creative Space

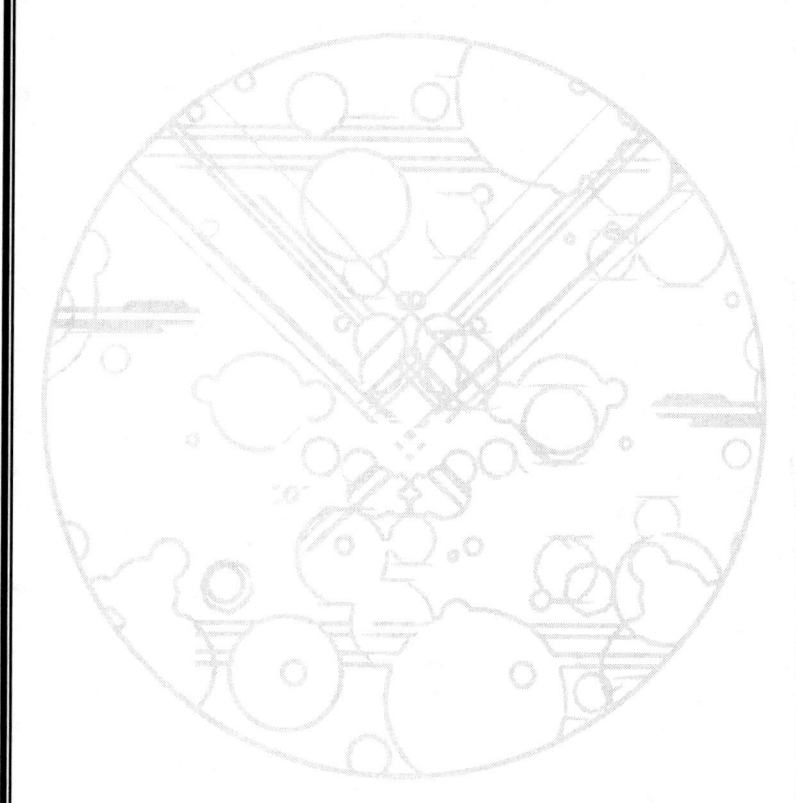

A little quiet time alone with our thoughts can help our brain to calm and focus. Use this Creative Space to write out thoughts or ideas you have (don't judge thoughts or ideas as good or bad, just free-think, you can even write the craziest things you can think of!) Drawing or coloring has been shown to have a therapeutic, calming effect too.

Day by day, in every way I'm getting better and better.

My Gratitude Journal

"Do not spoil what you have by desiring what you have not; remember that what you now have was once among the things you only hoped for." Epicurus

Today's Date _____ and My Mood was 😊 😐 😑 😒 😬 😢 😶

Who or what made me smile today? 😊

Did I make someone smile or laugh today?

How was I kind today?

How did I help someone/something today, even in a small way?

What did I give today? Could be your time, knowledge, money, love, etc.

Today I am very grateful for having this person in my life and why:

I learned something new today:

Did I thank someone today? Who should I surprise by sending a card?

Of all the things I saw today the best by far was this: 👀

I gave someone this compliment today:

I am looking forward to this (it's OK if it's the same as yesterday!):

I would like to help:

I think this would be fun to try and maybe a bit scary:

Today I am grateful for: Anything, health, wealth, wisdom, fun, a feeling

Remembering, My goal going forward is to:

Day by day, in every way I'm getting better and better.

Creative Space

A little quiet time alone with our thoughts can help our brain to calm and focus. Use this Creative Space to write out thoughts or ideas you have (don't judge thoughts or ideas as good or bad, just free-think, you can even write the craziest things you can think of!) Drawing or coloring has been shown to have a therapeutic, calming effect too.

Day by day, in every way I'm getting better and better.

My Gratitude Journal

"Whatever you appreciate and give thanks for will increase in your life."
Sanaya Roman

Today's Date _____ and My Mood was

I'm very good at:

What I like about _____ is:

What I am most proud of is:

My favorite thing about Me is my:

Today, I smiled because

I am so lucky I can, or get to:

I'm grateful for:

If I lost everything else, I'd still be grateful for:

This made me happy today:

_____ always makes me smile.

I would like to help:

When I think of _____ it makes me feel good.

My favorite _____ is _____ because

Remembering, My goal going forward is to:

Day by day, in every way I'm getting better and better.

Creative Space

A little quiet time alone with our thoughts can help our brain to calm and focus. Use this Creative Space to write out thoughts or ideas you have (don't judge thoughts or ideas as good or bad, just free-think, you can even write the craziest things you can think of!) Drawing or coloring has been shown to have a therapeutic, calming effect too.

Day by day, in every way I'm getting better and better.

My Gratitude Journal

"Take full account of what Excellencies you possess, and in gratitude remember how you would hanker after them, if you had them not." — Marcus Aurelius

Today's Date _____ and My Mood was

Who or what made me smile today?

Did I make someone smile or laugh today?

How was I kind today?

How did I help someone/something today, even in a small way?

What did I give today? Could be your time, knowledge, money, love, etc.

Today I am very grateful for having this person in my life and why:

I learned something new today:

Did I thank someone today? Who should I surprise by sending a card?

Of all the things I saw today the best by far was this:

I gave someone this compliment today:

I am looking forward to this (it's OK if it's the same as yesterday!):

I would like to help:

I think this would be fun to try and maybe a bit scary:

Today I am most grateful for:

Remembering, My goal going forward is to:

Day by day, in every way I'm getting better and better. 43

Creative Space

A little quiet time alone with our thoughts can help our brain to calm and focus. Use this Creative Space to write out thoughts or ideas you have (don't judge thoughts or ideas as good or bad, just free-think, you can even write the craziest things you can think of!) Drawing or coloring has been shown to have a therapeutic, calming effect too.

Day by day, in every way I'm getting better and better.

My Gratitude Journal

"Gratitude is the ability to experience life as a gift. It liberates us from the prison of self-preoccupation." John Ortberg

Today's Date _____ and My Mood was 🙂 😐 😕 😒 😠 😢 ⭕

I'm very good at:

What I like about _____ is:

What I am most proud of is:

My favorite thing about Me is my:

Today, I smiled because

I am so lucky I can, or get to:

I'm grateful for:

If I lost everything else, I'd still be grateful for:

This made me happy today:

_____ always makes me smile.

I would like to help:

When I think of _____ it makes me feel good.

My favorite _____ is _____ because

Remembering, My goal going forward is to:

Day by day, in every way I'm getting better and better.

Creative Space

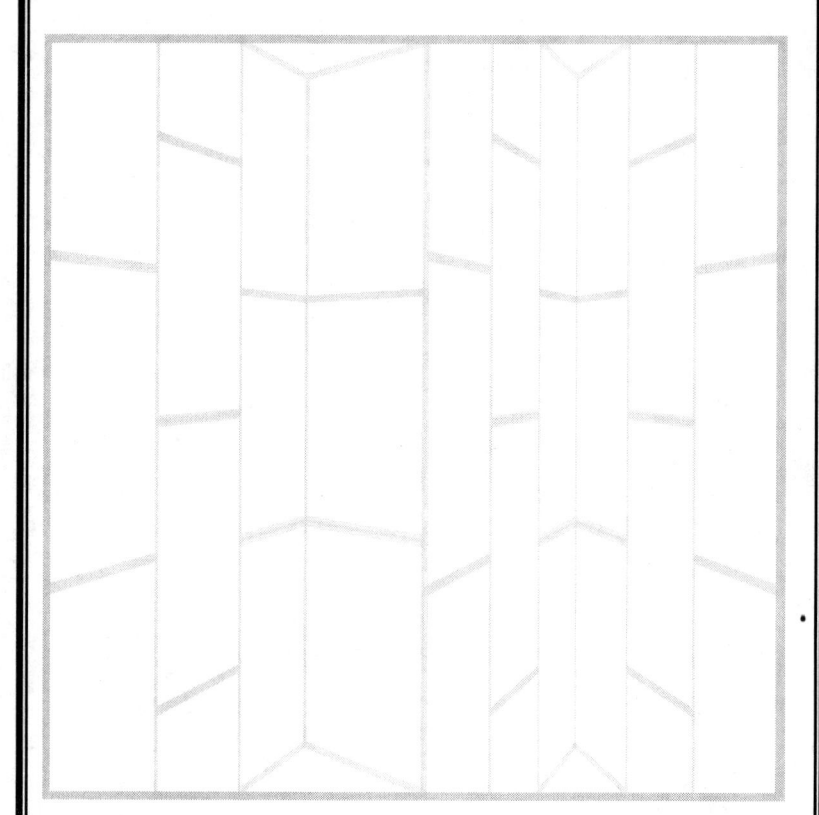

A little quiet time alone with our thoughts can help our brain to calm and focus. Use this Creative Space to write out thoughts or ideas you have (don't judge thoughts or ideas as good or bad, just free-think, you can even write the craziest things you can think of!) Drawing or coloring has been shown to have a therapeutic, calming effect too.

Day by day, in every way I'm getting better and better.

My Gratitude Journal

"I may not be where I want to be, but I'm thankful for not being where I used to be." — Habeeb Akande

Today's Date _____ and My Mood was

Who or what made me smile today?

Did I make someone smile or laugh today?

How was I kind today?

How did I help someone/something today, even in a small way?

What did I give today? Could be your time, knowledge, money, love, etc.

Today I am very grateful for having this person in my life and why:

I learned something new today:

Did I thank someone today? Who should I surprise by sending a card?

Of all the things I saw today the best by far was this:

I gave someone this compliment today:

I am looking forward to this (it's OK if it's the same as yesterday!):

I would like to help:

I think this would be fun to try and maybe a bit scary:

Today I am grateful for: Anything, health, wealth, wisdom, fun, a feeling

Remembering, My goal going forward is to:

Day by day, in every way I'm getting better and better.

Creative Space

A little quiet time alone with our thoughts can help our brain to calm and focus. Use this Creative Space to write out thoughts or ideas you have (don't judge thoughts or ideas as good or bad, just free-think, you can even write the craziest things you can think of!) Drawing or coloring has been shown to have a therapeutic, calming effect too.

Day by day, in every way I'm getting better and better.

Little Things

A summer's breeze, a smiling child,
A daffodil that's growing wild,
A deep orange sunset in the West;
Those little things, I love the best.

A still dark night with fireflies,
The laughter in my mother's eyes,
A multicolored rainbow's end...
Are little things that count, my friend.

A fuzzy warm puppy (licking my face),
Kisses with hugs and a loving embrace,
Rain pouring down on a roof made of tin,
Sitting under a shade (with soft gentle wind);

Those little things make life worth living.
Being kind to a stranger, caring and giving,
Laughing and sharing your hopes and your dreams;
There is nothing more precious than the little things.

Vicky Lamdin

Creative Space

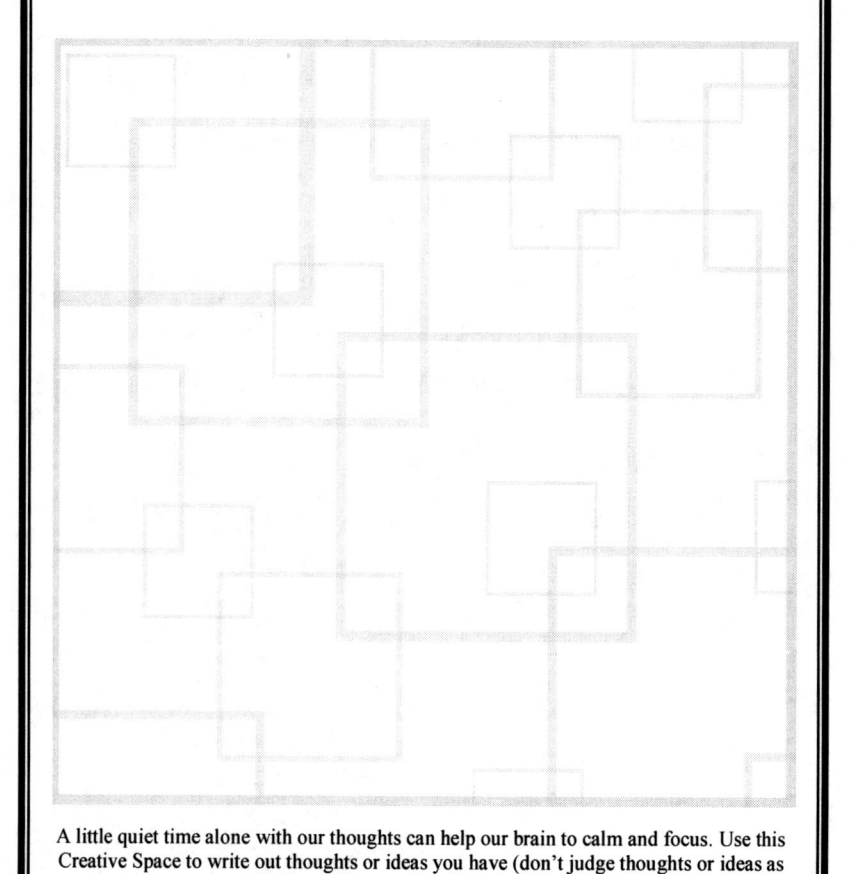

A little quiet time alone with our thoughts can help our brain to calm and focus. Use this Creative Space to write out thoughts or ideas you have (don't judge thoughts or ideas as good or bad, just free-think, you can even write the craziest things you can think of!) Drawing or coloring has been shown to have a therapeutic, calming effect too.

Day by day, in every way I'm getting better and better.

My Gratitude Journal

"Gratitude for the seemingly insignificant—a seed—this plants the giant miracle."
Ann Voskamp

Today's Date _____ and My Mood was 🙂 😐 😑
                                            😕 😬 😢

Who or what made me smile today? 🙂

Did I make someone smile or laugh today?

How was I kind today?

How did I help someone/something today, even in a small way?

What did I give today? Could be your time, knowledge, money, love, etc.

Today I am very grateful for having this person in my life and why:

I learned something new today:

Did I thank someone today? Who should I surprise by sending a card?

Of all the things I saw today the best by far was this: 👀

I gave someone this compliment today:

I am looking forward to this (it's OK if it's the same as yesterday!):

I would like to help:

I think this would be fun to try and maybe a bit scary:

Today I am grateful for: Anything, health, wealth, wisdom, fun, a feeling

Remembering, My goal going forward is to:

Day by day, in every way I'm getting better and better.

Creative Space

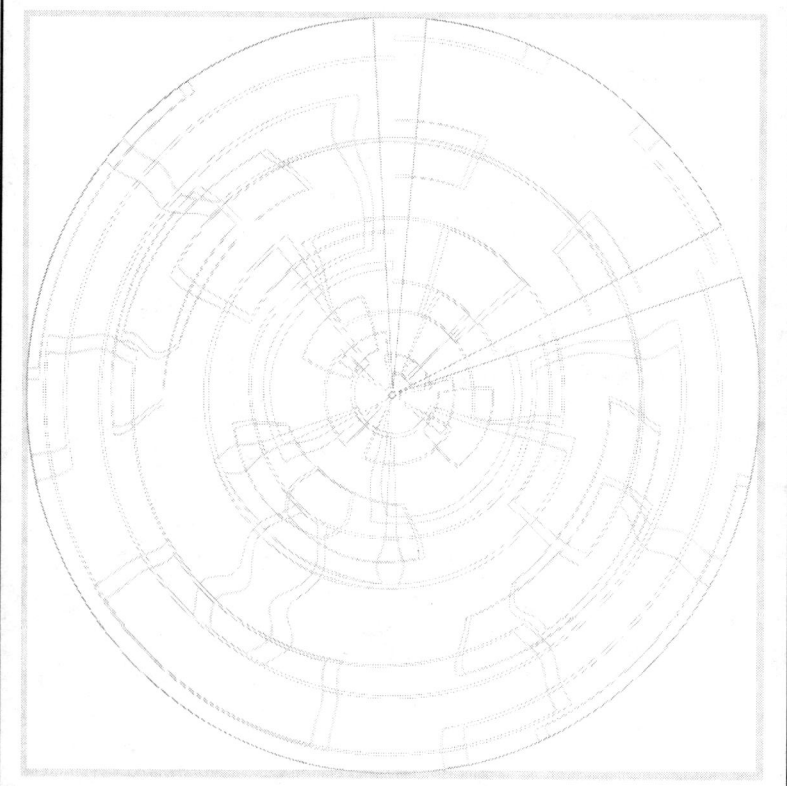

A little quiet time alone with our thoughts can help our brain to calm and focus. Use this Creative Space to write out thoughts or ideas you have (don't judge thoughts or ideas as good or bad, just free-think, you can even write the craziest things you can think of!) Drawing or coloring has been shown to have a therapeutic, calming effect too.

Day by day, in every way I'm getting better and better.

My Gratitude Journal

"Gratitude always comes into play; research shows that people are happier if they are grateful for the positive things in their lives, rather than worrying about what might be missing." Dan Buettner

Today's Date _____ and My Mood was

I am so lucky I can, or get to:

Today, I smiled because

What I like about _____ is:

What I am most proud of is:

When I think of _____ it makes me feel good.

My favorite thing about Me is my:

I'm grateful for:

This made me happy today:

I find it easy to:

_____ always makes me smile.

I would like to help:

If I lost everything else, I'd still be grateful for:

My favorite _____ is _____ because

Today, I'm most grateful for:

Remembering, My goal going forward is to:

Day by day, in every way I'm getting better and better.

Creative Space

A little quiet time alone with our thoughts can help our brain to calm and focus. Use this Creative Space to write out thoughts or ideas you have (don't judge thoughts or ideas as good or bad, just free-think, you can even write the craziest things you can think of!) Drawing or coloring has been shown to have a therapeutic, calming effect too.

Day by day, in every way I'm getting better and better.

My Gratitude Journal

"When you express gratitude for the blessings that come into your life, it not only encourages the universe to send you more, it also sees to it that those blessings remain." Stephen Richards

Today's Date _____ and My Mood was

Who or what made me smile today?

Did I make someone smile or laugh today?

How was I kind today?

How did I help someone/something today, even in a small way?

What did I give today? Could be your time, knowledge, money, love, etc.

Today I am very grateful for having this person in my life and why:

I learned something new today:

Did I thank someone today? Who should I surprise by sending a card?

Of all the things I saw today the best by far was this:

I gave someone this compliment today:

I am looking forward to this (it's OK if it's the same as yesterday!):

I would like to help:

I think this would be fun to try and maybe a bit scary:

Today I am grateful for: Anything, health, wealth, wisdom, fun, a feeling

My goal to focus on right now is:

Day by day, in every way I'm getting better and better.

Creative Space

A little quiet time alone with our thoughts can help our brain to calm and focus. Use this Creative Space to write out thoughts or ideas you have (don't judge thoughts or ideas as good or bad, just free-think, you can even write the craziest things you can think of!) Drawing or coloring has been shown to have a therapeutic, calming effect too.

Day by day, in every way I'm getting better and better.

My Gratitude Journal

"Whatever we think about and thank about we bring about."
John F. Demartini

Today's Date _____ and My Mood was

I'm super-good at:

I am so lucky I can, or get to:

What I like about _____ is:

What I am most proud of is:

My favorite thing about Me is my:

Today, I smiled because

I'm grateful for:

This made me happy today:

_____ always makes me smile.

I would like to help:

When I think of _____ it makes me feel good.

If I lost everything else, I'd still be grateful for:

My favorite _____ is _____ because

Today, I'm most grateful for:

Remembering, My goal going forward is to:

Day by day, in every way I'm getting better and better.

Creative Space

A little quiet time alone with our thoughts can help our brain to calm and focus. Use this Creative Space to write out thoughts or ideas you have (don't judge thoughts or ideas as good or bad, just free-think, you can even write the craziest things you can think of!) Drawing or coloring has been shown to have a therapeutic, calming effect too.

Day by day, in every way I'm getting better and better.

My Gratitude Journal

"If a fellow isn't thankful for what he's got, he isn't likely to be thankful for what he's going to get." Frank A. Clark

Today's Date _____ and My Mood was

Who or what made me smile today?

Did I make someone smile or laugh today?

How was I kind today?

How did I help someone/something today, even in a small way?

What did I give today? Could be your time, knowledge, money, love, etc.

Today I am very grateful for having this person in my life and why:

I learned something new today:

Did I thank someone today? Who should I surprise by sending a card?

Of all the things I saw today the best by far was this:

I gave someone this compliment today:

I am looking forward to this (it's OK if it's the same as yesterday!):

I would like to help:

I think this would be fun to try and maybe a bit scary:

Today I am grateful for: Anything, health, wealth, wisdom, fun, a feeling

Other Notes:

Day by day, in every way I'm getting better and better.

Creative Space

A little quiet time alone with our thoughts can help our brain to calm and focus. Use this Creative Space to write out thoughts or ideas you have (don't judge thoughts or ideas as good or bad, just free-think, you can even write the craziest things you can think of!) Drawing or coloring has been shown to have a therapeutic, calming effect too.

Day by day, in every way I'm getting better and better.

My Gratitude Journal

"He is a wise man who does not grieve for the things which he has not, but rejoices for those which he has." Epictetus

Today's Date _____ and My Mood was

I'm very good at:

What I like about _____ is:

What I am most proud of is:

My favorite thing about Me is my:

Today, I smiled because

I am so lucky I can, or get to:

I'm grateful for:

If I lost everything else, I'd still be grateful for:

This made me happy today:

_____ always makes me smile.

I would like to help:

When I think of _____ it makes me feel good.

My favorite _____ is _____ because

Remembering, My goal going forward is to:

Day by day, in every way I'm getting better and better.

Creative Space

A little quiet time alone with our thoughts can help our brain to calm and focus. Use this Creative Space to write out thoughts or ideas you have (don't judge thoughts or ideas as good or bad, just free-think, you can even write the craziest things you can think of!) Drawing or coloring has been shown to have a therapeutic, calming effect too.

Day by day, in every way I'm getting better and better.

My Gratitude Journal

"The deepest craving of human nature is the need to be appreciated." William James
Who did you appreciate today? Did you tell them?

Today's Date _____ and My Mood was 😊 😐 😠
                                              😒 😬 😢

Who or what made me smile today? 😊

Did I make someone smile or laugh today?

How was I kind today?

How did I help someone/something today, even in a small way?

What did I give today? Could be your time, knowledge, money, love, etc.

Today I am very grateful for having this person in my life and why:

I learned something new today:

Did I thank someone today? Who should I surprise by sending a card?

Of all the things I saw today the best by far was this: 👀

I gave someone this compliment today:

I am looking forward to this (it's OK if it's the same as yesterday!):

I would like to help:

I think this would be fun to try and maybe a bit scary:

Today I am grateful for: Anything, health, wealth, wisdom, fun, a feeling

Other Notes:

Day by day, in every way I'm getting better and better.

Creative Space

A little quiet time alone with our thoughts can help our brain to calm and focus. Use this Creative Space to write out thoughts or ideas you have (don't judge thoughts or ideas as good or bad, just free-think, you can even write the craziest things you can think of!) Drawing or coloring has been shown to have a therapeutic, calming effect too.

Day by day, in every way I'm getting better and better.

My Gratitude Journal

"Be thankful for what you have; you'll end up having more. If you concentrate on what you don't have, you will never, ever have enough." Oprah Winfrey

Today's Date _____ and My Mood was 😊 🙂 😐 😒 😣 😢 ○

People say I'm good at:

What I like about _____ is:

I am most proud of my:

The thing I like about Me is:

Today, I smiled because

I am so lucky I can, or get to:

I'm grateful for:

If I lost everything else, I'd still be grateful for:

This made me happy today:

_____ always makes me smile.

I would like to help:

When I think of _____ it makes me feel good.

My favorite _____ is _____ because

Remembering, My goal going forward is to:

Day by day, in every way I'm getting better and better.

Creative Space

A little quiet time alone with our thoughts can help our brain to calm and focus. Use this Creative Space to write out thoughts or ideas you have (don't judge thoughts or ideas as good or bad, just free-think, you can even write the craziest things you can think of!) Drawing or coloring has been shown to have a therapeutic, calming effect too.

Day by day, in every way I'm getting better and better.

My Gratitude Journal

"It is impossible to feel grateful and depressed in the same moment."
Naomi Williams

Today's Date _____ and My Mood was

Who or what made me smile today?

Did I make someone smile or laugh today?

How was I kind today?

How did I help someone/something today, even in a small way?

What did I give today? Could be your time, knowledge, money, love, etc.

Today I am very grateful for having this person in my life and why:

I learned something new today:

Did I thank someone today? Who should I surprise by sending a card?

Of all the things I saw today the best by far was this:

I gave someone this compliment today:

I am looking forward to this (it's OK if it's the same as yesterday!):

I would like to help:

I think this would be fun to try and maybe a bit scary:

Today I am grateful for: Anything, health, wealth, wisdom, fun, a feeling

Other Notes:

Day by day, in every way I'm getting better and better.

Creative Space

A little quiet time alone with our thoughts can help our brain to calm and focus. Use this Creative Space to write out thoughts or ideas you have (don't judge thoughts or ideas as good or bad, just free-think, you can even write the craziest things you can think of!) Drawing or coloring has been shown to have a therapeutic, calming effect too.

Day by day, in every way I'm getting better and better.

My Gratitude Journal

"The only people with whom you should try to get even, are those who have helped you."
John E. Southard

Today's Date _____ and My Mood was

I am so lucky I can, or get to:

Today, I smiled because

What I like about _____ is:

What I am most proud of is:

When I think of _____ it makes me feel good.

My favorite thing about Me is my:

I'm grateful for:

This made me happy today:

I find it easy to:

_____ always makes me smile.

I would like to help:

If I lost everything else, I'd still be grateful for:

My favorite _____ is _____ because

Today, I'm most grateful for:

Remembering, My goal going forward is to:

Day by day, in every way I'm getting better and better.

Creative Space

A little quiet time alone with our thoughts can help our brain to calm and focus. Use this Creative Space to write out thoughts or ideas you have (don't judge thoughts or ideas as good or bad, just free-think, you can even write the craziest things you can think of!) Drawing or coloring has been shown to have a therapeutic, calming effect too.

Day by day, in every way I'm getting better and better.

My Gratitude Journal

"Gratitude and attitude are not challenges; they are choices."
Robert Braathe

Today's Date _____ and My Mood was

Who or what made me smile today?

Did I make someone smile or laugh today?

How was I kind today?

How did I help someone/something today, even in a small way?

What did I give today? Could be your time, knowledge, money, love, etc.

Today I am very grateful for having this person in my life and why:

I learned something new today:

Did I thank someone today? Who should I surprise by sending a card?

Of all the things I saw today the best by far was this:

I gave someone this compliment today:

I am looking forward to this (it's OK if it's the same as yesterday!):

I would like to help:

I think this would be fun to try and maybe a bit scary:

Today I am grateful for: Anything, health, wealth, wisdom, fun, a feeling

Other Notes:

Day by day, in every way I'm getting better and better.   71

Creative Space

A little quiet time alone with our thoughts can help our brain to calm and focus. Use this Creative Space to write out thoughts or ideas you have (don't judge thoughts or ideas as good or bad, just free-think, you can even write the craziest things you can think of!) Drawing or coloring has been shown to have a therapeutic, calming effect too.

Day by day, in every way I'm getting better and better.

My Gratitude Journal

"Let us be grateful to people who make us happy; they are the charming gardeners who make our souls blossom." Marcel Proust

Today's Date _____ and My Mood was

I am so lucky I can, or that I get to:

Today, I smiled because

What I like about _____ is:

What I am most proud of is:

When I think of _____ it makes me feel good.

My favorite thing about Me is my:

I feel blessed because:

This made me happy today:

I find it easy to:

_____ always makes me smile.

I would like to help:

If I lost everything else, I'd still be grateful for:

My favorite _____ is _____ because

Today, I'm most grateful for:

Remembering, My goal going forward is to:

Day by day, in every way I'm getting better and better.

73

Creative Space

A little quiet time alone with our thoughts can help our brain to calm and focus. Use this Creative Space to write out thoughts or ideas you have (don`t judge thoughts or ideas as good or bad, just free-think, you can even write the craziest things you can think of!) Drawing or coloring has been shown to have a therapeutic, calming effect too.

Day by day, in every way I'm getting better and better.

My Gratitude Journal

"We can only be said to be alive in those moments when our hearts are conscious of our treasures." Thornton Wilder

Today's Date _____ and My Mood was

Who or what made me smile today?

Did I make someone smile or laugh today?

How was I kind today?

How did I help someone/something today, even in a small way?

What did I give today? Could be your time, knowledge, money, love, etc.

Today I am very grateful for having this person in my life and why:

I learned something new today:

Did I thank someone today? Who should I surprise by sending a card?

Of all the things I saw today the best by far was this:

I gave someone this compliment today:

I am looking forward to this (it's OK if it's the same as yesterday!):

I would like to help:

I think this would be fun to try and maybe a bit scary:

Today I am most grateful for:

My goal is to ultimately:

Day by day, in every way I'm getting better and better.　　75

Creative Space

Let's Smile!

A little quiet time alone with our thoughts can help our brain to calm and focus. Use this Creative Space to write out thoughts or ideas you have (don't judge thoughts or ideas as good or bad, just free-think, you can even write the craziest things you can think of!) Drawing or coloring has been shown to have a therapeutic, calming effect too.

Day by day, in every way I'm getting better and better.

My Gratitude Journal

"There are only two ways to live your life. One is as though nothing is a miracle. The other is as though everything is a miracle." Albert Einstein

Today's Date _____ and My Mood was 😊 🙂 😐 😒 😬 😢 ⚪

One skill I have is:

What I like about _____ is:

What I am most proud of is:

My favorite thing about Me is my:

Today, I smiled because

I am so lucky I can, or get to:

I have the coolest thing, it's:

If I lost everything else, I'd still be grateful for:

This made me happy today:

_____ always makes me smile.

I would like to help:

When I think of _____ it makes me feel good.

My favorite _____ is _____ because

Remembering, My goal going forward is to:

Day by day, in every way I'm getting better and better.

Creative Space

A little quiet time alone with our thoughts can help our brain to calm and focus. Use this Creative Space to write out thoughts or ideas you have (don't judge thoughts or ideas as good or bad, just free-think, you can even write the craziest things you can think of!) Drawing or coloring has been shown to have a therapeutic, calming effect too.

Day by day, in every way I'm getting better and better.

My Gratitude Journal

"Gratitude can transform common days into thanksgivings, turn routine jobs into joy, and change ordinary opportunities into blessings." William Arthur Ward

Today's Date _____ and My Mood was

Who or what made me smile today?

Did I make someone smile or laugh today?

How was I kind today?

How did I help someone/something today, even in a small way?

What did I give today? Could be your time, knowledge, money, love, etc.

Today I am very grateful for having this person in my life and why:

I learned something new today:

Did I thank someone today? Who should I surprise by sending a card?

Of all the things I saw today the best by far was this:

I gave someone this compliment today:

I am looking forward to this (it's OK if it's the same as yesterday!):

I would like to help:

I think this would be fun to try and maybe a bit scary:

Today I am grateful for: Anything, health, wealth, wisdom, fun, a feeling

My most important goal right now is:

Day by day, in every way I'm getting better and better.

Creative Space

A little quiet time alone with our thoughts can help our brain to calm and focus. Use this Creative Space to write out thoughts or ideas you have (don't judge thoughts or ideas as good or bad, just free-think, you can even write the craziest things you can think of!)

My Gratitude Journal

"Reflect upon your present blessings, of which every man has plenty; not on your past misfortunes of which all men have some." Charles Dickens

Today's Date _____ and My Mood was

My favorite thing about Me is my:

I'm very good at:

What I like about _____ is:

This made me happy today:

What I am most proud of is:

Today, I smiled because

I am so lucky I can, or get to:

I'm grateful for:

If I lost everything else, I'd still be grateful for:

_____ always makes me smile.

I would like to help:

When I think of _____ it makes me feel good.

My favorite _____ is _____ because

Remembering, My goal going forward is to:

Day by day, in every way I'm getting better and better.

Creative Space

A little quiet time alone with our thoughts can help our brain to calm and focus. Use this Creative Space to write out thoughts or ideas you have (don't judge thoughts or ideas as good or bad, just free-think, you can even write the craziest things you can think of!) Drawing or coloring has been shown to have a therapeutic, calming effect too.

Day by day, in every way I'm getting better and better.

My Gratitude Journal

"Gratitude is riches. Complaint is poverty."
Doris Day

Today's Date _____ and My Mood was

Who or what made me smile today?

Did I make someone smile or laugh today?

How was I kind today?

How did I help someone/something today, even in a small way?

What did I give today? Could be your time, knowledge, money, love, etc.

Today I am very grateful for having this person in my life and why:

I learned something new today:

Did I thank someone today? Who should I surprise by sending a card?

Of all the things I saw today the best by far was this:

I gave someone this compliment today:

I am looking forward to this (it's OK if it's the same as yesterday!):

I would like to help:

I think this would be fun to try and maybe a bit scary:

Today I am grateful for:

This goal is most important to my progress right now:

Day by day, in every way I'm getting better and better.

Creative Space

A little quiet time alone with our thoughts can help our brain to calm and focus. Use this Creative Space to write out thoughts or ideas you have (don't judge thoughts or ideas as good or bad, just free-think, you can even write the craziest things you can think of!) Drawing or coloring has been shown to have a therapeutic, calming effect too.

Day by day, in every way I'm getting better and better.

My Gratitude Journal

"Many people who order their lives rightly in all other ways are kept in poverty by their lack of gratitude." Wallace Wattles

Today's Date _____ and My Mood was 🙂 😐 😕 😠 😬 😢 ○

My favorite thing about Me is my:

I'm very good at:

What I like about _____ is:

This made me happy today:

What I am most proud of is:

Today, I smiled because

I am so lucky I can, or get to:

I'm grateful for:

How do I want to grow:

_____ always makes me smile.

What do I want to contribute to the Planet:

When I think of _____ it makes me feel good.

What do I want to experience:

I should be focused on THIS goal at THIS time:

Smile With Me!

Day by day, in every way I'm getting better and better.   85

Creative Space

A little quiet time alone with our thoughts can help our brain to calm and focus. Use this Creative Space to write out thoughts or ideas you have (don't judge thoughts or ideas as good or bad, just free-think, you can even write the craziest things you can think of!) Drawing or coloring has been shown to have a therapeutic, calming effect too.

Day by day, in every way I'm getting better and better.

My Gratitude Journal

"One kind word can warm three winter months."
Japanese proverb

Today's Date _____ and My Mood was

Who or what made me smile today?

Did I make someone smile or laugh today?

How was I kind today?

How did I help someone/something today, even in a small way?

What did I give today? Could be your time, knowledge, money, love, etc.

Today I am very grateful for having this person in my life and why:

I learned something new today:

Did I thank someone today? Who should I surprise by sending a card?

Of all the things I saw today the best by far was this:

I gave someone this compliment today:

I am looking forward to this (it's OK if it's the same as yesterday!):

I would like to help:

I think this would be fun to try and maybe a bit scary:

Today I am grateful for:

My most important goal is:

Day by day, in every way I'm getting better and better. 87

Creative Space

A little quiet time alone with our thoughts can help our brain to calm and focus. Use this Creative Space to write out thoughts or ideas you have (don`t judge thoughts or ideas as good or bad, just free-think, you can even write the craziest things you can think of!) Drawing or coloring has been shown to have a therapeutic, calming effect too.

Day by day, in every way I'm getting better and better.

My Gratitude Journal

"The best way to cheer yourself up is to cheer someone else up."
Mark Twain

Today's Date _____ and My Mood was

I'm very good at:

What I like about _____ is:

This made me happy today:

What I am most proud of is:

Today, I smiled because

I am so lucky I can, or get to:

My favorite thing about Me is my:

I'm grateful for _____ today, because:

How do I want to grow:

_____ always makes me smile.

What do I want to contribute to the Planet:

When I think of _____ it makes me feel good.

What do I want to experience:

Remembering, My goal going forward is to:

Day by day, in every way I'm getting better and better.

Creative Space

A little quiet time alone with our thoughts can help our brain to calm and focus. Use this Creative Space to write out thoughts or ideas you have (don't judge thoughts or ideas as good or bad, just free-think, you can even write the craziest things you can think of!) Drawing or coloring has been shown to have a therapeutic, calming effect too.

Day by day, in every way I'm getting better and better.

My Gratitude Journal

"Be happy while you're living. For you're a long time dead."
Scottish Proverb

Today's Date _____ and My Mood was

Who or what made me smile today?

Did I make someone smile or laugh today?

How was I kind today?

How did I help someone/something today, even in a small way?

What did I give today? Could be your time, knowledge, money, love, etc.

Today I am very grateful for having this person in my life and why:

I learned something new today:

Did I thank someone today? Who should I surprise by sending a card?

Of all the things I saw today the best by far was this:

I gave someone this compliment today:

I am looking forward to this (it's OK if it's the same as yesterday!):

I would like to help:

I think this would be fun to try and maybe a bit scary:

Today I am grateful for:

My focus right now should be on this goal:

Day by day, in every way I'm getting better and better.   91

Creative Space

A little quiet time alone with our thoughts can help our brain to calm and focus. Use this Creative Space to write out thoughts or ideas you have (don't judge thoughts or ideas as good or bad, just free-think, you can even write the craziest things you can think of!) Drawing or coloring has been shown to have a therapeutic, calming effect too.

Day by day, in every way I'm getting better and better.

My Gratitude Journal

"Don't cry because it's over, smile because it happened."
Author Unknown

Today's Date _____ and My Mood was

My favorite thing about Me is my:

I'm very good at:

What I like about _____ is:

This made me happy today:

What I am most proud of is:

Today, I smiled because

I am so lucky I can, or get to:

I'm grateful for:

How do I want to grow:

_____ always makes me smile.

What do I want to contribute to the Planet:

When I think of _____ it makes me feel good.

What do I want to experience:

I should be focused on THIS goal at THIS time:

Day by day, in every way I'm getting better and better.

Creative Space

A little quiet time alone with our thoughts can help our brain to calm and focus. Use this Creative Space to write out thoughts or ideas you have (don't judge thoughts or ideas as good or bad, just free-think, you can even write the craziest things you can think of!) Drawing or coloring has been shown to have a therapeutic, calming effect too.

Day by day, in every way I'm getting better and better.

My Gratitude Journal

"Every day may not be good, but there's something good in every day."
Author Unknown

Today's Date _____ and My Mood was

Who or what made me smile today?

Did I make someone smile or laugh today?

How was I kind today?

How did I help someone/something today, even in a small way?

What did I give today? Could be your time, knowledge, money, love, etc.

Today I am very grateful for having this person in my life and why:

I learned something new today:

Did I thank someone today? Who should I surprise by sending a card?

Of all the things I saw today the best by far was this:

I gave someone this compliment today:

I am looking forward to this (it's OK if it's the same as yesterday!):

I would like to help:

I think this would be fun to try and maybe a bit scary:

Today I am grateful for:

This is my most important goal to focus on now:

Day by day, in every way I'm getting better and better.

Creative Space

A little quiet time alone with our thoughts can help our brain to calm and focus. Use this Creative Space to write out thoughts or ideas you have (don't judge thoughts or ideas as good or bad, just free-think, you can even write the craziest things you can think of!) Drawing or coloring has been shown to have a therapeutic, calming effect too.

Day by day, in every way I'm getting better and better.

My Gratitude Journal

"The unthankful heart discovers no mercies; but the thankful heart will find, in every hour, some heavenly blessings." Henry Ward Beecher

Today's Date _____ and My Mood was

Today, I smiled because

Today I made _____ smile or laugh.

What I am most proud of about me is:

I am so lucky I can, or get to:

I'm very good at:

What I like about _____ is:

This made me happy today:

I'm grateful for:

How do I want to grow:

_____ always makes me smile.

What do I want to contribute to:

When I think of _____ it makes me feel good.

What do I want to experience:

I should be focused on THIS goal at THIS time:

Day by day, in every way I'm getting better and better.

Creative Space

A little quiet time alone with our thoughts can help our brain to calm and focus. Use this Creative Space to write out thoughts or ideas you have (don't judge thoughts or ideas as good or bad, just free-think, you can even write the craziest things you can think of!) Drawing or coloring has been shown to have a therapeutic, calming effect too.

My Gratitude Journal

"Success is not something you pursue; it's something you attract by who you become."
Jim Rohn

Today's Date _____ and My Mood was

Who or what made me smile today?

Did I make someone smile or laugh today?

How was I kind today?

How did I help someone/something today, even in a small way?

What did I give today? Could be your time, knowledge, money, love, etc.

Today I am very grateful for having this person in my life and why:

I learned something new today:

Did I thank someone today? Who should I surprise by sending a card?

Of all the things I saw today the best by far was this:

I gave someone this compliment today:

I am looking forward to this (it's OK if it's the same as yesterday!):

I would like to help:

I think this would be fun to try and maybe a bit scary:

Today I am grateful for:

The goal I am most eager to accomplish is:

Day by day, in every way I'm getting better and better.

Creative Space

BE PROUD!

A little quiet time alone with our thoughts can help our brain to calm and focus. Use this Creative Space to write out thoughts or ideas you have (don't judge thoughts or ideas as good or bad, just free-think, you can even write the craziest things you can think of!) Drawing or coloring has been shown to have a therapeutic, calming effect too.

Day by day, in every way I'm getting better and better.

My Gratitude Journal

"Life doesn't get better by chance, it gets better by choice."
Jim Rohn

Today's Date _____ and My Mood was 😊 😐 😑 😒 😠 😢 ⭕

Today, I smiled because

Today I made _____ smile or laugh.

What I am most proud of about me is:

I am so lucky I can, or get to:

I'm very good at:

What I like about _____ is:

This made me happy today:

I'm grateful for:

How do I want to grow:

_____ always makes me smile.

What do I want to contribute to:

When I think of _____ it makes me feel good.

What do I want to experience:

I should be focused on THIS goal at THIS time:

Day by day, in every way I'm getting better and better.

101

Creative Space

A little quiet time alone with our thoughts can help our brain to calm and focus. Use this Creative Space to write out thoughts or ideas you have (don't judge thoughts or ideas as good or bad, just free-think, you can even write the craziest things you can think of!) Drawing or coloring has been shown to have a therapeutic, calming effect too.

Day by day, in every way I'm getting better and better.

My Gratitude Journal

"A moment of gratitude makes a difference in your attitude."
Bruce Wilkenson

Today's Date _____ and My Mood was

Who or what made me smile today?

Did I make someone smile or laugh today?

How was I kind today?

How did I help someone/something today, even in a small way?

What did I give today? Could be your time, knowledge, money, love, etc.

Today I am very grateful for having this person in my life and why:

I learned something new today:

Did I thank someone today? Who should I surprise by sending a card?

Of all the things I saw today the best by far was this:

I gave someone this compliment today:

I am looking forward to this (it's OK if it's the same as yesterday!):

I would like to help:

I think this would be fun to try and maybe a bit scary:

Today I am grateful for:

My most important goal to achieve is:

Day by day, in every way I'm getting better and better.

Creative Space

A little quiet time alone with our thoughts can help our brain to calm and focus. Use this Creative Space to write out thoughts or ideas you have (don't judge thoughts or ideas as good or bad, just free-think, you can even write the craziest things you can think of!) Drawing or coloring has been shown to have a therapeutic, calming effect too.

Day by day, in every way I'm getting better and better.

My Gratitude Journal

"As we express our gratitude, we must never forget that the highest appreciation is not to utter the words, but to live by them." John F. Kennedy

Today's Date _____ and My Mood was

Today, I smiled because

Today I made _____ smile or laugh.

What I am most proud of about me is:

I am so lucky I can, or get to:

I'm very good at:

What I like about _____ is:

This made me happy today:

I'm grateful for:

How do I want to grow:

_____ always makes me smile.

What do I want to contribute to:

When I think of _____ it makes me feel good.

What do I want to experience:

I should be focused on THIS goal at THIS time:

Day by day, in every way I'm getting better and better.

Creative Space

A little quiet time alone with our thoughts can help our brain to calm and focus. Use this Creative Space to write out thoughts or ideas you have (don't judge thoughts or ideas as good or bad, just free-think, you can even write the craziest things you can think of!) Drawing or coloring has been shown to have a therapeutic, calming effect too.

Day by day, in every way I'm getting better and better.

My Gratitude Journal

"Gratitude is not only the greatest of virtues, but the parent of all others."
Cicero

Today's Date _____ and My Mood was

Who or what made me smile today?

Did I make someone smile or laugh today?

How was I kind today?

How did I help someone/something today, even in a small way?

What did I give today? Could be your time, knowledge, money, love, etc.

Today I am very grateful for having this person in my life and why:

I learned something new today:

Did I thank someone today? Who should I surprise by sending a card?

Of all the things I saw today the best by far was this:

I gave someone this compliment today:

I am looking forward to this (it's OK if it's the same as yesterday!):

I would like to help:

I think this would be fun to try and maybe a bit scary:

Today I am grateful for: Anything, health, wealth, wisdom, fun, a feeling

Concentrate on this goal now:

Day by day, in every way I'm getting better and better.   107

Let's Smile!

Creative Space

A little quiet time alone with our thoughts can help our brain to calm and focus. Use this Creative Space to write out thoughts or ideas you have (don't judge thoughts or ideas as good or bad, just free-think, you can even write the craziest things you can think of!) Drawing or coloring has been shown to have a therapeutic, calming effect too.

Day by day, in every way I'm getting better and better.

My Gratitude Journal

"The miracle of gratitude is that it shifts your perception to such an extent that it changes the world you see." Dr. Robert Holden

Today's Date _____ and My Mood was

Today, I smiled when:

Today I made _____ smile or laugh.

What I am most proud of about me is:

I am so lucky I can, or get to:

I'm very good at:

What I like about my _____ is:

I feel happiest when I:

I'm grateful for:

How do I want to grow:

_____ always makes me smile.

What do I want to contribute to:

Thinking of _____ makes me feel good.

What do I want to experience:

I should be focused on THIS goal at THIS time:

Day by day, in every way I'm getting better and better.

Creative Space

A little quiet time alone with our thoughts can help our brain to calm and focus. Use this Creative Space to write out thoughts or ideas you have (don't judge thoughts or ideas as good or bad, just free-think, you can even write the craziest things you can think of!) Drawing or coloring has been shown to have a therapeutic, calming effect too.

Day by day, in every way I'm getting better and better.

My Gratitude Journal

"It doesn't matter if the glass is half empty or half full; be grateful you have a glass and there is something in it."
Mark Cuban

Today's Date _____ and My Mood was

Who or what made me smile today?

Did I make someone smile or laugh today?

How was I kind today?

How did I help someone/something today, even in a small way?

What did I give today? Could be your time, knowledge, money, love, etc.

Today I am very grateful for having this person in my life and why:

I learned something new today:

Did I thank someone today? Who should I surprise by sending a card?

Of all the things I saw today the best by far was this:

I gave someone this compliment today:

I am looking forward to this (it's OK if it's the same as yesterday!):

I would like to help:

I think this would be fun to try and maybe a bit scary:

Today I am grateful for: Anything, health, wealth, wisdom, fun, a feeling

Remembering, my goal is :

Day by day, in every way I'm getting better and better.

Creative Space

A little quiet time alone with our thoughts can help our brain to calm and focus. Use this Creative Space to write out thoughts or ideas you have (don't judge thoughts or ideas as good or bad, just free-think, you can even write the craziest things you can think of!) Drawing or coloring has been shown to have a therapeutic, calming effect too.

Day by day, in every way I'm getting better and better.

My Gratitude Journal

"When we give cheerfully and accept gratefully, everyone is blessed."
Maya Angelou

Today's Date _____ and My Mood was

Today, I smiled when:

Today I made _____ smile or laugh.

What I am most proud of about me is:

I am so lucky I can, or get to:

I'm very good at:

What I like about my _____ is:

I feel happiest when I:

I'm grateful for:

How do I want to grow:

_____ always makes me smile.

What do I want to contribute to:

Thinking of _____ makes me feel good.

What do I want to experience:

I should be focused on THIS goal at THIS time:

Day by day, in every way I'm getting better and better.

Creative Space

A little quiet time alone with our thoughts can help our brain to calm and focus. Use this Creative Space to write out thoughts or ideas you have (don't judge thoughts or ideas as good or bad, just free-think, you can even write the craziest things you can think of!) Drawing or coloring has been shown to have a therapeutic, calming effect too.

Day by day, in every way I'm getting better and better.

My Gratitude Journal

"Be grateful for what you have; work hard for what you don't."
Unknown

Today's Date _____ and My Mood was

Who or what made me smile today?

Did I make someone smile or laugh today?

How was I kind today?

How did I help someone/something today, even in a small way?

What did I give today? Could be your time, knowledge, money, love, etc.

Today I am very grateful for having this person in my life and why:

I learned something new today:

Did I thank someone today? Who should I surprise by sending a card?

Of all the things I saw today the best by far was this:

I gave someone this compliment today:

I am looking forward to this (it's OK if it's the same as yesterday!):

I would like to help:

I think this would be fun to try and maybe a bit scary:

Today I am grateful for: Anything, health, wealth, wisdom, fun, a feeling

My biggest goal right now is:

Day by day, in every way I'm getting better and better.

Creative Space

A little quiet time alone with our thoughts can help our brain to calm and focus. Use this Creative Space to write out thoughts or ideas you have (don't judge thoughts or ideas as good or bad, just free-think, you can even write the craziest things you can think of!)

Day by day, in every way I'm getting better and better.

My Gratitude Journal

"Silent gratitude isn't much use to anyone."
Gladys Browyn Stern

Today's Date _____ and My Mood was 😊 🙂 😐 😒 😡 😢

Today, I smiled when:

Today I made _____ smile or laugh.

What I am most proud of about me is:

I am so lucky I can, or get to:

I'm very good at:

What I like about my _____ is:

I feel happiest when I:

I'm grateful for:

How do I want to grow:

_____ always makes me smile.

What do I want to contribute to:

Thinking of _____ makes me feel good.

What do I want to experience:

I should be focused on THIS goal at THIS time:

Day by day, in every way I'm getting better and better.

Creative Space

A little quiet time alone with our thoughts can help our brain to calm and focus. Use this Creative Space to write out thoughts or ideas you have (don't judge thoughts or ideas as good or bad, just free-think, you can even write the craziest things you can think of!) Drawing or coloring has been shown to have a therapeutic, calming effect too.

Day by day, in every way I'm getting better and better.

My Gratitude Journal

"Let us be grateful to people who make us happy; they are the charming gardeners who make our souls blossom." Marcel Proust

Today's Date _____ and My Mood was

Who or what made me smile today?

Did I make someone smile or laugh today?

How was I kind today?

How did I help someone/something today, even in a small way?

What did I give today? Could be your time, knowledge, money, love, etc.

Today I am very grateful for having this person in my life and why:

I learned something new today:

Did I thank someone today? Who should I surprise by sending a card?

Of all the things I saw today the best by far was this:

I gave someone this compliment today:

I am looking forward to this (it's OK if it's the same as yesterday!):

I would like to help:

I think this would be fun to try and maybe a bit scary:

Today I am grateful for: Anything, health, wealth, wisdom, fun, a feeling

I must hold this goal as a priority right now:

Day by day, in every way I'm getting better and better.

Creative Space

A little quiet time alone with our thoughts can help our brain to calm and focus. Use this Creative Space to write out thoughts or ideas you have (don't judge thoughts or ideas as good or bad, just free-think, you can even write the craziest things you can think of!) Drawing or coloring has been shown to have a therapeutic, calming effect too.

Day by day, in every way I'm getting better and better.

My Gratitude Journal

"Gratitude makes sense of our past, brings peace for today and creates a vision for tomorrow."
Melody Beattie

Today's Date _____ and My Mood was 🙂 😐 😑
                                              😒 😬 😟

Who or what made me smile today? 🙂

Did I make someone smile or laugh today?

How was I kind today?

How did I help someone/something today, even in a small way?

What did I give today? Could be your time, knowledge, money, love, etc.

Today I am very grateful for having this person in my life and why:

I learned something new today:

Did I thank someone today? Who should I surprise by sending a card?

Of all the things I saw today the best by far was this: 👀

I gave someone this compliment today:

I am looking forward to this (it's OK if it's the same as yesterday!):

I would like to help:

I think this would be fun to try and maybe a bit scary:

Today I am grateful for: Anything, health, wealth, wisdom, fun, a feeling

Goals are my roadmap for life. Where am I heading now:

Day by day, in every way I'm getting better and better.

Creative Space

A little quiet time alone with our thoughts can help our brain to calm and focus. Use this Creative Space to write out thoughts or ideas you have (don't judge thoughts or ideas as good or bad, just free-think, you can even write the craziest things you can think of!) Drawing or coloring has been shown to have a therapeutic, calming effect too.

Day by day, in every way I'm getting better and better.

My Gratitude Journal

"A miracle happened: another day of life."
Paulo Coelho

Today's Date _____ and My Mood was

Who or what made me smile today?

Did I make someone smile or laugh today?

How was I kind today?

How did I help someone/something today, even in a small way?

What did I give today? Could be your time, knowledge, money, love, etc.

Today I am very grateful for having this person in my life and why:

I learned something new today:

Did I thank someone today? Who should I surprise by sending a card?

Of all the things I saw today the best by far was this:

I gave someone this compliment today:

I am looking forward to this (it's OK if it's the same as yesterday!):

I would like to help:

I think this would be fun to try and maybe a bit scary:

Today I am grateful for: Anything, health, wealth, wisdom, fun, a feeling

Written goals have power. My goal is:

Day by day, in every way I'm getting better and better.

Creative Space

YOU ARE AMAZING!

A little quiet time alone with our thoughts can help our brain to calm and focus. Use this Creative Space to write out thoughts or ideas you have (don't judge thoughts or ideas as good or bad, just free-think, you can even write the craziest things you can think of!) Drawing or coloring has been shown to have a therapeutic, calming effect too.

Day by day, in every way I'm getting better and better.

My Gratitude Journal

"At times our own light goes out and is rekindled by a spark from another person. Pause to think with deep gratitude of those who have lighted the flame within us." Albert Schweitzer

Today's Date _____ and My Mood was

Today, I smiled when:

Today I made _____ smile or laugh.

What I am most proud of about me is:

I am so lucky I can, or get to:

I'm very good at:

What I like about my _____ is:

I feel happiest when I:

I'm grateful for:

How do I want to grow:

_____ always makes me smile.

What do I want to contribute to:

Thinking of _____ makes me feel good.

What do I want to experience:

I should be focused on THIS goal at THIS time:

Day by day, in every way I'm getting better and better.

Creative Space

A little quiet time alone with our thoughts can help our brain to calm and focus. Use this Creative Space to write out thoughts or ideas you have (don't judge thoughts or ideas as good or bad, just free-think, you can even write the craziest things you can think of!) Drawing or coloring has been shown to have a therapeutic, calming effect too.

Day by day, in every way I'm getting better and better.

My Gratitude Journal

"Gratitude is the path to wisdom, the escape to self-peace and the nourishment of happiness."
Marinela Reka

Today's Date _____ and My Mood was

Who or what made me smile today?

Did I make someone smile or laugh today?

How was I kind today?

How did I help someone/something today, even in a small way?

What did I give today? Could be your time, knowledge, money, love, etc.

Today I am very grateful for having this person in my life and why:

I learned something new today:

Did I thank someone today? Who should I surprise by sending a card?

Of all the things I saw today the best by far was this:

I gave someone this compliment today:

I am looking forward to this (it's OK if it's the same as yesterday!):

I would like to help:

I think this would be fun to try and maybe a bit scary:

Today I am grateful for: Anything, health, wealth, wisdom, fun, a feeling

I must focus on this goal, right now:

Day by day, in every way I'm getting better and better.

Creative Space

YOU'RE NICE!
HAVE A BONE

A little quiet time alone with our thoughts can help our brain to calm and focus. Use this Creative Space to write out thoughts or ideas you have (don't judge thoughts or ideas as good or bad, just free-think, you can even write the craziest things you can think of!) Drawing or coloring has been shown to have a therapeutic, calming effect too.

Day by day, in every way I'm getting better and better.

My Gratitude Journal

"The happiest people do not necessarily have the best of everything, but make the best of everything they have."
Unknown

Today's Date _____ and My Mood was

Who or what made me smile today?

Did I make someone smile or laugh today?

How was I kind today?

How did I help someone/something today, even in a small way?

What did I give today? Could be your time, knowledge, money, love, etc.

Today I am very grateful for having this person in my life and why:

I learned something new today:

Did I thank someone today? Who should I surprise by sending a card?

Of all the things I saw today the best by far was this:

I gave someone this compliment today:

I am looking forward to this (it's OK if it's the same as yesterday!):

I would like to help:

I think this would be fun to try and maybe a bit scary:

Today I am grateful for: Anything, health, wealth, wisdom, fun, a feeling

My highest priority (my goal right now) is:

Day by day, in every way I'm getting better and better.

Creative Space

A little quiet time alone with our thoughts can help our brain to calm and focus. Use this Creative Space to write out thoughts or ideas you have (don't judge thoughts or ideas as good or bad, just free-think, you can even write the craziest things you can think of!) Drawing or coloring has been shown to have a therapeutic, calming effect too.

Day by day, in every way I'm getting better and better.

My Gratitude Journal

"At the end of each day you should play back the tapes of your performance. The results should either applaud or prod you." Jim Rohn

Today's Date _____ and My Mood was

Today, this made me smile:

Today I made _____ smile or laugh.

I think I have a great:

I am so lucky I can, or get to:

I'm very good at:

What I like about my_____ is:

I feel happiest when I:

I'm grateful for:

Other people admire my:

_____ always makes me smile.

What do I want to contribute to:

Thinking of _____ makes me feel good.

What do I want to experience:

I should be focused on THIS goal at THIS time:

Day by day, in every way I'm getting better and better.   131

Creative Space

A little quiet time alone with our thoughts can help our brain to calm and focus. Use this Creative Space to write out thoughts or ideas you have (don't judge thoughts or ideas as good or bad, just free-think, you can even write the craziest things you can think of!) Drawing or coloring has been shown to have a therapeutic, calming effect too.

Day by day, in every way I'm getting better and better.

My Gratitude Journal

"There is no better opportunity to receive more, than to be thankful for what you already have." Jim Rohn

Today's Date _____ and My Mood was

Who or what made me smile today?

Did I make someone smile or laugh today?

How was I kind today?

How did I help someone/something today, even in a small way?

What did I give today? Could be your time, knowledge, money, love, etc.

Today I am very grateful for having this person in my life and why:

I learned something new today:

Did I thank someone today? Who should I surprise by sending a card?

Of all the things I saw today the best by far was this:

I gave someone this compliment today:

I am looking forward to this (it's OK if it's the same as yesterday!):

I would like to help:

I think this would be fun to try and maybe a bit scary:

Today I am grateful for:

Goals attract our future. My goal is:

Day by day, in every way I'm getting better and better.   133

Creative Space

I WILL 'MERRY' YOU!

A little quiet time alone with our thoughts can help our brain to calm and focus. Use this Creative Space to write out thoughts or ideas you have (don't judge thoughts or ideas as good or bad, just free-think, you can even write the craziest things you can think of!) Drawing or coloring has been shown to have a therapeutic, calming effect too.

Day by day, in every way I'm getting better and better.

My Gratitude Journal

"Do not spoil what you have by wishing for what you have not; but remember that what you have now was once among the things you only hoped for." Epictetus

Today's Date _____ and My Mood was

Today, I smiled when:

Today I made _____ smile or laugh.

What I am most proud of about me is:

I am so lucky I can, or get to:

I'm very good at:

What I like about my _____ is:

I feel happiest when I:

I'm grateful for:

How do I want to grow:

_____ always makes me smile.

What do I want to contribute to:

Thinking of _____ makes me feel good.

I want to experience:

I should be focused on THIS goal at THIS time:

Day by day, in every way I'm getting better and better.

Creative Space

A little quiet time alone with our thoughts can help our brain to calm and focus. Use this Creative Space to write out thoughts or ideas you have (don't judge thoughts or ideas as good or bad, just free-think, you can even write the craziest things you can think of!) Drawing or coloring has been shown to have a therapeutic, calming effect too.

Day by day, in every way I'm getting better and better.

My Gratitude Journal

"We can complain because rose bushes have thorns,
or rejoice because thorn bushes have roses." Abraham Lincoln

Today's Date _____ and My Mood was

Who or what made me smile today?

Did I make someone smile or laugh today?

How was I kind today?

How did I help someone/something today, even in a small way?

What did I give today? Could be your time, knowledge, money, love, etc.

Today I am very grateful for having this person in my life and why:

I learned something new today:

Did I thank someone today? Who should I surprise by sending a card?

Of all the things I saw today the best by far was this:

I gave someone this compliment today:

I am looking forward to this (it's OK if it's the same as yesterday!):

I would like to help:

I think this would be fun to try and maybe a bit scary:

Today I am grateful for: Anything, health, wealth, wisdom, fun, a feeling

Remembering, my goal going forward is to

Day by day, in every way I'm getting better and better.

YOU DID IT!

Creative Space

A little quiet time alone with our thoughts can help our brain to calm and focus. Use this Creative Space to write out thoughts or ideas you have (don't judge thoughts or ideas as good or bad, just free-think, you can even write the craziest things you can think of!) Drawing or coloring has been shown to have a therapeutic, calming effect too.

Day by day, in every way I'm getting better and better.

My Gratitude Journal

Congratulations!

You are a special person.

The rare individual who can finish what they start.

You are a person of dedication and discipline.

Discipline is the bridge that takes us over the challenges that lie between what we want and what we don't have yet.

Keep up the good work.
Keep journaling.
Keep coloring.
Keep growing.

Don't stop now...

Get Your Volume 2 Journal at:
http://JournalOnUp.com

Here's a FREE Space!

Tip: You can write anything you like here, or draw, or just leave it blank for now so you can look back on this several years from now and note your new thoughts. Or, this might be a good place to now record any changes you've noticed since you began working with the journal - sort of a before and after thing. It's your free page...it's all up to you!

My Gratitude Journal

"Happiness cannot be traveled to, owned, earned, worn or consumed. Happiness is the spiritual experience of living every minute with love, grace and gratitude." Denis Waitley

Why Mandalas Make Us Feel Good

The word Mandala comes from the ancient Sanskrit language and translates to 'sacred circle' or 'center'.

Circles appear throughout nature in flowers, snowflakes the sun, the moon, and planets. Man has used circles in architecture and design from the beginning of time as powerful symbols in cultures throughout world history.

According to the University of New Hampshire Health Science Department, Tibetan Buddhist Monks and Native American Indian tribes have all used mandalas as a way of evoking spiritual energy, meditation and healing. More recently, the renowned psychologist Carl Jung used mandalas with his clients and discovered the act of creating mandalas allowed a deep healing to take place from within the human psyche.

In just the last 5 years, adults coloring mandalas has become very popular as we seek to de-stress and find escape from the many inputs of the modern world.

What can you expect to gain from coloring mandalas?

- Relaxation
- Centering of mind and spirit
- Expansion of your creativity
- Increased focus and concentration
- Have fun - alone or with family or friends
- Connect with kids and release your inner child too
- Lifts your spirits
- The joy of creating a unique work of art
- Activate the intuitive genius within

read more ▶

Day by day, in every way I'm getting better and better.

My Gratitude Journal

"Comparison is the thief of joy"
Theodore Roosevelt

How To Color a Mandala

While there is no right or wrong way to color a mandala, (using your intuition and creativity is half the fun!) there are a few tips we have found that produce the best results:

Use crayons or colored pencils, because markers or ink pens tend to bleed through the paper causing problems for the back side of the page. Have your crayons or pencils handy before you begin so you don't get up and down.

Find quiet time when you can be uninterrupted - coloring mandalas provides the greatest benefit when you can concentrate or focus exclusively on the activity from start to finish.

Breathe to Relax First - you can expect the most from this activity when you are relaxed before you begin. Focus on your breathing to start. Close your eyes. Now slowly inhale through your nose as you count to four. Hold briefly, then exhale slowly through your mouth as you count to eight. Four in. Eight out. Repeat until you feel relaxed.

Don't judge as you color, just do. Have fun. Create!

*While not all of the designs in this book fit the strict circular definition of a mandala, the concentrated act of coloring and creating art always produces a relaxing, calming influence over the mind and body. I hope you enjoy working with the unique designs I have created for you. Most were created using my design tool of choice, Photoshop You can find additional and larger manadalas to color for **FREE** at:

http://JournalOnUp.com

Day by day, in every way I'm getting better and better.

My Gratitude Journal

About the Author

Robert Schwarztrauber is an award-winning photographer, author, and creator of numerous digital and physical books sold around the world. Robert's specialty is writing books that help people do things better while having more fun in the process.

In addition to being a photographer and published author, Robert also shows those who want to write and publish their own books how to do it quickly and easily. He has a system you might like.

His website, **http://bookwritingmagic.com** has many free tips and resources for those who want to fulfill their dream of writing and publishing a book of their own, for fun, business, or a legacy.

Robert is also an accomplished speaker and freely shares his knowledge, insights and tips with audiences who wish to learn, laugh and grow from the experience and stories he shares.

Robert has personally designed all of the graphics, images and mandalas specifically for this book. His hope is that the mandalas bring peace and harmony to your life, the words and questions will inspire and build your self-confidence and self-esteem, and that the zany, smiley-faced characters sprinkled throughout the pages will lift your spirits and maybe make you laugh just a little.

"Everything in this book has been included because it helped me. I hope it will help you too!"

Robert Schwarztrauber

Find us on [f]

http://facebook.com/thegratitudedude